THE CHASTENING
OF THE LORD

THE CHASTENING
OF THE LORD

by

Frederick K.C. Price, Ph.D.

FAITH ONE
PUBLISHING
LOS ANGELES, CALIFORNIA

The Chastening of the Lord
ISBN 1-883798-10-8
Copyright © 1995 by
Frederick K.C. Price, Ph.D.
P.O. Box 90000
Los Angeles, CA 90009

Published by Faith One Publishing
7901 South Vermont Avenue
Los Angeles, California 90044

Contents

Contents

Introduction

The chastening of the Lord — what is it, and what is it not? Some Christians, and even non-Christians, have concluded that God uses troubles and trials, sickness and disease to chasten His children. They have the idea that the Lord puts these things on them to make better people out of them.

Is this really true? Does God really do this, and does He do it to make better people out of us? And if God does not send calamities our way, how does He chasten us?

To fully learn the answers to these questions, we must go to the source of this subject — God's Word — and learn for ourselves what exactly the chastening of the Lord really is, and what it truly entails. This way, we can know exactly what to expect from God, and what the devil may send our way in the guise of our being chastened.

1

What Is Chastening?

Hebrews 12:1-11:

Therefore we also, since we are surrounded by so great a cloud of witnesses, let us lay aside every weight, and the sin which so easily ensnares us, and let us run with endurance [or patience, as the King James Bible puts it] the race that is set before us,

looking unto Jesus, the author and finisher of our faith, who for the joy that was set before Him endured the cross, despising the shame, and has sat down at the right hand of the throne of God.

For consider Him who endured such hostility from sinners against Himself, lest you become weary and discouraged in your souls.

You have not yet resisted to bloodshed, striving against sin.

And you have forgotten the exhortation which speaks to you as to sons: "My son, do not despise the chastening of the Lord, Nor be discouraged when you are rebuked by Him;

For whom the Lord loves He chastens, And scourges every son whom He receives.

If you endure chastening, God deals with you as sons; for what son is there whom a father does not chasten?

But if you are without chastening, of which all have become partakers, then you are illegitimate and not sons.

1

> Furthermore, we have had human fathers who
> corrected us, and we paid them respect. Shall we not
> much more readily be in subjection to the Father of
> spirits and live?
> For they indeed for a few days chastened us as
> seemed best to them, but He for our profit, that we
> may be partakers of His holiness.
> Now no chastening seems to be joyful for the
> present, but painful; nevertheless, afterward it yields
> the peaceable fruit of righteousness to those who
> have been trained by it.

One of the primary challenges we have had in learning about the chastening of the Lord has been a misunderstanding in the meaning of the word *chasten*. In the twelfth chapter of Hebrews, this word literally means "to child-train." It does not mean "punishment." God does not punish His children, but He will chastise them.

If you look up the word *chastisement* in the English dictionary, you will notice that it means "to punish." We have assumed that *chasten* has the same meaning in the Greek that it has in English. It does not. This misunderstanding is partly to blame for the idea that God punishes His children with trials, tribulations, sickness, disease, and other calamities, all for the purpose of making better people out of them.

A Rewarder, Not a Punisher

Many people have thought that God was punishing them for something they had done in the past. Some people will not even come into the family of God for fear that

God will get them for all the bad things they have done through the years. They are scared. By "scared," I do not mean a reverential fear, but scared in the same way they may be frightened of a rattlesnake or a monster.

Let us look at some things that will help us understand the chastening of the Lord more clearly. If you do not understand how God chastens us, you will not be able to use your faith. You will be terrified, and, consequently, your faith will not work. So you need to understand what the chastening of the Lord really is. Once you find that out, you will love to be chastised — but you have to have your mind changed about what the word *chasten* really means.

Paul writes in Hebrews 11:6:

> **But without faith it is impossible to please Him, for he who comes to God must believe that He is, and that He is a rewarder of those who diligently seek Him.**

You cannot exercise your faith, or even muster up faith to believe God for anything, if you are scared He will hit you over the head with something every time you make a mistake in life. You will actually be unconsciously afraid to use your faith. And without faith, you cannot please God.

If you decide to operate by faith, you have to believe that God is a rewarder and that He is not after you or trying to get back at you for any reason. Many people have a fear of God, and it is unfounded, according to the Word.

Actually, the Lord does not have to punish you. Your disobedience to His Word will do that. Getting out of line with God's Word will place you in a position to be bombed out by the devil. Satan, technically, is the punisher. Actually, he is trying to kill you, and that in itself is punishment.

That brings us back to the question, "If God's form of chastening is not punishment, what is it?"

As I said before, our challenge comes from not understanding what the word *chasten* really means. In Hebrews 12, this word, along with *chastisement*, means "to child-train." It means "to teach, to instruct, to train as in training a child in the way he should go." God does not punish to train you, and He does not put anything negative on you to make you a better person.

Another word which confirms *chastisement* as child-training is found in Hebrews 12:9:

> **Furthermore, we have had human fathers who corrected us, and we paid them respect. Shall we not much more readily be in subjection to the Father of spirits and live?**

The word *corrected*, or *corrector*, has two basic meanings. The first meaning is "teacher." The second meaning is "instructor" or "chastiser." A chastiser is a teacher or an instructor, not a punisher.

For Whom the Lord Loves

Think about this: Let us say God is the One who sends sickness, disease, and all the other negative things our way. If that were true, the reward of the

4

righteous would be trouble, trials, and tribulations, because Hebrews 12:6 tells us:

> **"For whom the Lord loves, He chastens, And scourges every son whom He receives."**

The key phrase here is *every son*. If the Lord loved all His children and sent all these negative things on them because they did something wrong, it would mean that no Christian would be exonerated in the sight of God. Every child of God would be afflicted with trials and tests simply because they were children of God. Everyone does something wrong once in a while, and according to Hebrews 12:6, God chastens and scourges every son.

Notice also that Hebrews 12:6 does not define or indicate what things you have to do wrong, or what scourging or chastening you will receive as a result of what you do. The verse simply says God scourges and chastens every son who comes to Him. That leaves it wide open as to what God could chasten and scourge you for.

However, in Hebrews 12:5, we have a statement which, if taken in the context I have just outlined, is rather curious:

> **And you have forgotten the exhortation which speaks to you as to sons: "My son, do not despise the chastening of the Lord, Nor be discouraged when you are rebuked by Him."**

The exhortation mentioned in this verse is found in Job 5:17, which says:

"Behold, happy is the man whom God corrects; Therefore do not despise the chastening of the Almighty."

If we think of chastisement as punishment, as we do in the English language, there is nothing to be happy about when you are punished. However, these verses encourage us to be happy when we are chastened. You cannot be happy when you have cancer. You cannot rejoice when your finances are going down the tubes, or when anything else is having a negative impact on your life.

It sounds more like chastening in these verses has something to do with correcting, not punishing. That would square with the definition of *chasten* we described earlier — namely, "to teach, instruct, train as you would train up a child."

How do you train up a child? You would not teach a child to stay away from a hot burner on the stove by placing the child's hand on the burner, and saying, "That will teach you. Never put your hand on a hot stove." If any parent did that, he or she would be guilty of child abuse.

We have traditionally accused God of putting sickness, disease, or calamity on us to train us. That is what churches and ministers have been saying: "The Lord is testing you. The Lord is training you." You know what that would be in our society? You know what they would arrest you for? Child abuse. Yet we have accused God of doing just that. Paul brings up another point in Hebrews 12:7.

> **If you endure chastening, God deals with you as with sons; for what son is there whom a father does not chasten?**

"*If*" is the qualifier here, and it indicates something very important. It indicates that you have a decision to make as to whether or not to endure the chastening. When sickness or disease comes upon you, you have no choice about whether or not you will endure it. Most of us would choose not to have it come within 27,000 miles of us.

We have a choice as to whether or not to endure chastening. This means chastening must be none of the things God has traditionally been accused of doing, because you have no choice when those things happen to you. You can refuse to submit to God's training, and there is always a negative consequence as a result; however, God has nothing to do with that. As I already stated, God does not punish you, nor does He have to. God wants to train you, but He cannot do it if you do not allow Him to.

Hebrews 12:7 goes on to say that if we endure chastening, God will deal with us as sons, **for what son is there whom a father does not chasten?** You would not be considered a good parent if you had five children, and trained only one of them. Therefore, God endeavors to train all of His children.

Jesus gives us a further indication of God's attitude toward Believers in Matthew 7:7-11:

> "Ask, and it will be given to you; seek, and you will find; knock, and it will be opened to you.
> "For everyone who asks receives, and he who seeks finds, and to him who knocks it will be opened.
> "Or what man is there among you who, if his son asks for bread, will give him a stone?
> "Or if he asks for a fish, will he give him a serpent?
> "If you then, being evil, know how to give good gifts to your children, how much more will your Father who is in heaven give good things to those who ask Him!"

Jesus is saying that God is a better father to us than we are parents to our own children. I have never given my children a stone when they asked for bread. I have never given them a snake when they asked for a fish. Jesus tells us, **"If you then, being evil, know how to give good gifts to your children, how much more will your Father who is in heaven give good things to those who ask Him!"**

Notice, Jesus says that God gives good things. Sickness, disease, and other bad news are not good things. Therefore, God could not have anything to do with them.

Some people have also claimed that God uses negative things to get us to repent. That is not scripturally true. Romans 2:1-4 tells us:

> Therefore you are inexcusable, O man, whoever you are who judge, for in whatever you judge another you condemn yourself; for you who judge practice the same things.
> But we know that the judgment of God is according to truth against those who practice such things.

And do you think this, O man, you who judge those practicing such things, and doing the same, that you will escape the judgment of God?

Or do you despise the riches of His goodness, forbearance, and longsuffering, not knowing that the goodness of God leads you to repentance?

God leads you to repentance by His goodness, not by trials, tribulations, or calamities. God does not drive you to repentance. He leads you to it, after He has put up with you for a long time. God will not take anything away from you or do something bad to you to bring you into repentance. He will do something good for you, if you have enough sense to perceive it.

2

How God Chastens

The reason God chastens us is that He loves us. He wants us to succeed, to live the overcoming Christian life to the best of our abilities. Psalm 94:12 tells us,

**Blessed is the man whom You instruct, O Lord,
And teach out of Your law.**

We are supposed to be blessed when God chastens us. You are not blessed when your dog is killed, when you have cancer, when your business is destroyed, or when your finances are ripped off. When you are blessed, you receive something that will benefit you, that will make your life better, not worse.

We also read earlier that God is a rewarder of those who diligently seek Him. A reward, like a blessing, is something that will improve your general situation. Therefore, there is no way you could realistically construe anything negative as a reward.

When God teaches us, we are blessed. How, then, are we taught? The verse we just read spells it out in no uncertain terms:

**Blessed is the man whom You instruct, O Lord,
And teach out of Your law.**

The word *law* is a synonym for the Word of God. That is how God teaches and trains us — not by punishing us, not by putting cancer on us, not by killing your dog, destroying your business, or ripping off your finances. He trains us by His Word.

How does God get His Word to us? He does not just come down and do it personally. He does it through the ministry gifts He has placed in the Church. He does it in the local church, through the pastor, the apostle, the evangelist, the prophet, and the teacher, because that is where the Body of Christ gathers together. That is how God trains us, if we will submit to the authority He has placed in the Church.

The problem is, many people will not submit to authority. They may say, "I don't care what Fred Price says," but they are missing the whole point. They may think I am the one coming up with the things I say, but it is not me. It is the Word of the Lord.

Whipping Us in Love

The Lord wants to help us. He wants to teach us and train us to be winners in the things of God. However, chastening can hurt. This is why Hebrews 12:6 says,

> **"For whom the Lord loves He chastens, And scourges every son whom He receives."**

To *scourge* someone means "to whip" that individual. That is what they did to Jesus. The Bible says they scourged Him. When you whip someone, even if it is only by telling that person something that could save his life, it is going to hurt. That person may be grateful later that you took the time and effort to help, but initially, there may be some pain.

Every time God leads me to talk about people being overweight, it hurts the people God is trying to help, and they get angry about what I say. Those people are not getting angry at me. They are getting angry at God, because He is whipping them. He is not doing it to punish them, but that is the effect it has when they rebel against God's chastening. It is just like being whipped, and it hurts.

When I start talking about obesity, it hurts. When I start talking about murmuring and complaining, it hurts. When I talk about being late, or about being undependable, or about writing checks for the offering when there are insufficient funds to cover the checks, it hurts. You do not like being whipped, do you? It is painful. But God says through Paul that He scourges every son. He is training us, teaching us — His children — and that is how He does it — through His Word.

I get letters all the time from people who are upset. One woman wrote me a letter accusing me of being a "fat basher." Then she contacted a major television station that aired *Ever Increasing Faith*, and raised so much trouble that the people at the station said, "Look, that is a paid broadcast. They are paying for their broadcast. We have no control over what they are saying." After that, the station started putting in a disclaimer before each broadcast, saying they were not responsible for what was said on *Ever Increasing Faith*.

People like that woman do not realize what comes out of my mouth is part of the training. That is the chastening of the Lord, and they are murmuring and rebelling against it. It is God trying to help those people. He is constantly wanting to train and teach His children. But He cannot do it except through His vessels that He sets in the Church.

I do not like someone calling me a "fat basher." Those people who are overweight and get offended do not know I could be the best friend they ever had. I would be one of the few people who would really tell them the truth, and tell it to them in love — not to try to hurt them, but only to encourage them. Some of the physical problems these people have is a result of their being overweight. But who is going to talk about it? Most people would not do it, because they do not want to be called a "fat basher."

I do not like talking about obesity. I do not like upsetting people. However, I would rather have people mad at me, and God glad, than to have people glad and God mad. That, plus the fact it can possibly help someone in the process, is the bottom line.

One Sunday, I was led in the course of the service to minister in the Spirit. God gave me a word in other tongues, then the interpretation. In the interpretation, I said that someone in the congregation was not only overweight, but that it was now detrimental to that person's health. I said that in the Spirit. Nobody responded at the time, and I had no idea who the person was that I had talked about.

After the service, a woman came up to one of my daughters, and told her that she was the person I was talking about. She also said that what I had said was exactly what her doctor had told her that very week, and that what I said encouraged her to do something about it.

It was really the Lord who told her that in the service. I am not that smart, and I did not know this person's situation. But that was how the Lord wanted to do it. He attempts to help us every way that He can, and most of the time, most people will not receive His help. But He is going to do it through the Word. He is not going to do it through the circumstances. You may opt to learn something through the circumstances, but that is not the way God wants you to learn. He wants you to learn by His Word. It is much less painful, and you will not have to go through so much.

That is one reason God wants us filled with the Holy Spirit. When you are filled with the Holy Spirit, you will be open for God to give you the direction you need to help the people. I do not know what goes on in your house, behind closed doors, but God does. However, He is not going to come down here to do something about it. He will do it through the ministry gift that He sets in the Church.

When a minister is not filled with the Spirit, he does not have this insight. This is why many ministers do not say anything in the service that chastens people. How can they? They do not have the mind of the Spirit. They do not know what you, as an individual, are going through.

These ministers always try to say everything that sounds good to people, so the people will continue to come and give offerings to the church. The theory is, if you make people angry, they will not give an offering. So, most of the time, these preachers will say things that will placate the people — things that sound good, but have no real substance. That way, people do not get upset and quit coming to church.

I do not do that. I want to be obedient to the Lord, and I am surprised myself sometimes when I hear what comes out of my mouth. I think, "Oh, my God. Here I go again. I know I'm in trouble now." But I have a mandate from God, and it is the Spirit of God operating through me that is saying those things. God is not going to come down to earth and stand behind the pulpit to tell people what to do. If He did, you would listen to Him. You may think you have a legitimate excuse for not listening to me, because I am just a man. What can I know? But you had better learn how to discern the Spirit of God, or you are going to be in trouble.

Chastening Is Training

In 2 Timothy 3:16, we have this statement:

> **All Scripture is given by inspiration of God, and is profitable for doctrine, for reproof, for correction, for instruction in righteousness,**

The word *instruction* in this verse, in the Greek, is the same word translated as *chasten* in Hebrews 12. We could read 2 Timothy 3:16 like this:

**All Scripture is given by inspiration of God, and
is profitable for doctrine, for reproof, for correction,
for chastening in righteousness,**

Again, chastening is instruction. Instruction is not
punishment. Another facet of the chastening of the
Lord is found in Ephesians 6:4.

**And you, fathers, do not provoke your children
to wrath, but bring them up in the training and
admonition of the Lord.**

The word *training* in Ephesians is also the same
Greek word for *chasten* in Hebrews 12. "To train" is the
same as "to instruct," or "point in the right direction."
Training, instructing, and chastening all refer to the
same thing.

The easiest way to relate to this is to think about
faithfulness. God is teaching us all the time, through
His own faithfulness, about the fact that we should be
faithful. However, some people have heard the Word,
but they have not let it make contact with their spirits.
They are unfaithful to the things of God because their
word is not any good. Because of this, God cannot trust
these people. He loves them, but He cannot trust them.

When my children were very small, they would sit
in their high-chairs at dinner time, and sometimes
throw their little plastic cups on the floor. I never put
any crystal glasses in their hands when they were that
age. They could not handle anything so breakable.

Likewise, God cannot give some Christians some
things because they cannot handle them, even though

they have prayed and confessed that they have those items. God is a wise Father. He cannot allow those things to go to them, because they are not faithful. They would, in essence, throw those items on the floor, and break them.

There are people who have been saved 25 or 30 years and they still cannot be trusted. They may wonder, "How come God let so-and-so do that, and didn't let me do it?" They may not even be able to write their offering checks and have money in the bank to cover them. It goes back to the principle that he who is faithful in little will be faithful in much. If you cannot be trusted to do right with $5, why should God entrust you with $500,000?

The FaithDome cost $12 million to build, and the land it is on cost $14 million. That is $26 million altogether. God could trust me with that. I did not take a penny of it. It was not even a temptation to do so. You think God blessed this ministry with the money because Fred Price is so special? No. I would like to think I am special. I am special to my family. But I would be crazy to think I was God's special child, and God works through me just because I am Fred. God works through His children whom He can trust. I am on time. I keep my word. God wants to train you by having you do the little things in life. If you cannot be trusted with little things, you cannot be trusted with big things.

God wants us blessed. He wants us instructed. He wants us trained, so that when we grow up in Christ, we will be able to handle the responsibilities of kingdom living. He wants to entrust us with the things of God, but the way God is able to trust us is by our submitting to instruction. This is why some people are no further along in the things of the spirit than they are already. They have not submitted to the Word to be instructed by it. Because of that, they cannot be trusted.

Paul says in Hebrews 12:11:

> **Now no chastening seems to be joyful for the present, but painful; nevertheless, afterward it yields the peaceable fruit of righteousness to those who have been trained by it.**

The statement **have been trained by it** has the same basic meaning as, "It will produce for those who will submit to God's chastening." If you are not submitting to it, it will not produce. You can have all the books and all the tapes in the world, but that is not what makes this work. You have to be faithful to God's Word. That is how God will train and help you.

3

What About the Wilderness?

Some people say, "Well, Brother Price, sometimes the Lord will lead us through the wilderness to make us strong." It is one of those things we have heard and said that is unscriptural, but also traditional. The thing about it is, many people will believe an idea like that more than they will believe the Word of God. We need to look at some of these things, because it will help to free you up, especially if you have something from your past hanging over your head.

There are many people who think, "God will not forgive me of all the things I have done. All these bad things that are coming against my life are because of all the bad stuff I did back then." God does not remember you did anything bad once you come to Christ. I don't care if you killed 1,700 people — which I hope you have not done, and nobody should have that on his or her conscience. But no matter what you may have done, God will not hold it against you.

Let us say you murdered someone, or raped someone, or aborted or sold a child. You might have even given someone a disease that you knew you had. Yet, you interfaced with the person anyway, never saying

21

anything about it, and the person became infected with the disease. It is not good when people do any of those things, and you should not have done what you did. But you did it. It is over and done with. The bottle of milk is spilt, and you cannot put it back into the bottle, or put the bottle back together.

Once you come to Christ, God never remembers that you ever sinned, and He will not put something on you in the future to make you pay for something you did in the past. However, the devil will. Unfortunately, most preachers in the pulpit will cooperate with the devil by telling you, "Well, the Lord put that on you, brother [or sister]. God is testing and perfecting you. He is bringing you through the wilderness to make a better person out of you, and through it all, you will become strong in the things of the Lord."

That sounds reasonable, doesn't it? It seems like if we went through the wilderness, it would make us strong. Not according to the Bible. The Bible says that if you go through the wilderness, it will kill you graveyard dead. The children of Israel went through the wilderness for 40 years, and it did not make them strong. It killed every person 20 years old and upward except Caleb and Joshua.

Besides that, God Almighty did not put the children of Israel in the wilderness. They put themselves there, by their lack of faith and their unwillingness to follow God. They would not believe Him, and they would not receive what He had done for them. As a result, they had to go through the wilderness.

Many of the things you are putting up with are not things God has put into your life. In fact, the devil is not even putting those things on you. You are putting them on yourself. The devil is just seeing to it that they are enforced in your life, because you are on his turf, and he is going to try to break your head with all sorts of disasters.

However, a lot of negativity comes into your life because of your rebellion against doing what God says to do. You do not ever want to go through the "wilderness experience," because it can kill you.

In all of human history, if there were ever a case in point for what the wilderness experience can do to you, it would be the children of Israel. These Israelites had come out of Egypt, and God had worked miracles for them. They went through the Red Sea. The Egyptians were destroyed, and the children of Israel walked across an area of land called The Wilderness. They ended up on the banks of the Jordan River, looking into the land of Canaan.

God said to Moses, "Pick 12 men, one man out of each one of the tribes who is a leader of that tribe, and send them into the land to search it out. In other words, go spy out the land, and validate that it is exactly what I said it was — a land that flows with milk and honey." The 12 men were selected and sent out. They were gone 40 days before they finally returned.

Numbers 13:26-27:
Now they departed and came back to Moses and Aaron and all the congregation of the children of Israel in the Wilderness of Paran, at Kadesh; they brought back word to them and to all the congregation, and showed them the fruit of the land.

Then they told him, and said: "We went to the land where you sent us. It truly flows with milk and honey, and this is its fruit."

They did not say, "We think...." They did not say, "It seems to us that...." They did not say, "Our interpretation of it, Moses, is that..." They said, **"It truly flows with milk and honey, and this is its fruit."**

Numbers 13:28-33:

"Nevertheless the people who dwell in the land are strong; the cities are fortified and very large; moreover we saw the descendants of Anak there.

The Amalekites dwell in the land of the South; the Hittites, the Jebusites, and the Amorites dwell in the mountains; and the Canaanites dwell by the sea and along the banks of the Jordan."

Then Caleb quieted the people before Moses, and said, "Let us go up at once and take possession, for we are well able to overcome it."

But the men who had gone up with him said, "We are not able to go up against the people, for they are stronger than we."

And they gave the children of Israel a bad report of the land which they had spied out, saying, "The land through which we have gone as spies is a land that devours its inhabitants, and all the people whom we saw in it are men of great stature.

There we saw the giants (the descendants of Anak came from the giants); and we were like grasshoppers in our own sight, and so we were in their sight."

How did they know what they looked like to other people? They defeated themselves by saying they

24

could not take the land. God had said, "I give it to you," and they said, "We can't take it."

Complaining Is Evil, Unbelief a Sin

In Numbers 14, we have the sequel to this story.

Numbers 14:26-27:
And the Lord spoke to Moses and Aaron, saying, "How long shall I bear with this evil congregation who complain against Me?..."

You may think, because you do not commit fornication or adultery, or because you do not lie, smoke, steal, or gamble, that you are just fine with God. But God said, **"How long shall I bear with this evil congregation."** What did He call evil? The fact that they were out there committing adultery when they were out there those 40 days? The fact that they went out there and robbed banks those 40 days? The fact that they went out there and fire-bombed stores and looted different places? No. God said they brought back an evil report.

An evil report is a report of doubt. It is a report that refuses to believe that Almighty God is telling you the truth. It is a refusal to do things God's way.

Numbers 14:27-35:
"How long shall I bear with this evil congregation who complain against Me? I have heard the complaints which the children of Israel make against Me.

Say to them, 'As I live,' says the Lord, 'just as you have spoken in My hearing, so I will do to you:

'The carcasses of you who have complained against Me shall fall in this wilderness, all of you who were numbered, according to your entire number, from twenty years old and above.

'Except for Caleb the son of Jephunneh and Joshua the son of Nun, you shall by no means enter the land which I swore I would make you dwell in.

'But your little ones, whom you said would be victims, I will bring in, and they shall know the land which you have despised.

'But as for you, your carcasses shall fall in this wilderness.

'And your sons shall be shepherds in the wilderness forty years, and bear the brunt of your infidelity, until your carcasses are consumed in the wilderness.

'According to the number of the days in which you spied out the land, forty days, for each day you shall bear your guilt one year, namely forty years, and you shall know My rejection.

'I the Lord have spoken this. I will surely do so to all this evil congregation who are gathered together against Me. In this wilderness they shall be consumed, and there they shall die.'"

Notice, God told the people they would die in the wilderness, but it was not God who put them there. Their complaining against God and His servant, Moses, was what caused them to go into the wilderness. God's purpose for their going into the wilderness was not to make them strong. He said the people were going to die there. The people brought this disaster on themselves by their murmuring and complaining.

Notice also who heard the murmuring. In verse 27, God says, "I have heard." I have news for you. The Lord is still hearing. He has good batteries in His hearing aid, and they last forever. You may think it is all right to complain about the pastor if the man does not hear what you are saying, but the pastor is not the person you want to hide from. If anything, it would be better for you to say it to the pastor's face than to complain when he is not around and let God hear your complaining. All you do when you gripe and complain is to set yourself up for the wilderness.

God called the children of Israel's complaining evil. He said, **"How long shall I bear with this evil congregation who complain against Me?"** You may think that because you do not drink beer or cocktails, you do not smoke, you do not use drugs, and you do not lie or gamble, that it makes you all right. But you can go ahead and murmur and gripe, and that is just as much a sin before God as all those other things. That may be why your blessings have not come yet — because of your murmuring.

Notice something else that is absolutely awesome. All of the innocent were condemned because of the guilty. Caleb and Joshua believed God. They told the people they were well able to take the land. But they were cheated out of 40 years because of the people's murmuring.

The wilderness did not make the children of Israel strong. It killed every last one of the people who complained. I do not know about you, but I do not want to die, and I do not want to be prevented from going into the Promised Land because of murmuring. It would be better to have 300 people in the congregation who had a mind to do God's work and to do it His way than to have 10,000 people murmuring and complaining. That complaining will keep the blessing from the people who are doing things right.

If you do not like what a pastor is doing, the best thing for you to do is to get on your face before God, repent if you have been complaining, and start praying for the person. That is how you can change the situation, if you believe what he is doing is not of the Lord. If the pastor is doing what the Lord led him to do, and you leave yourself spiritually open, the Holy Spirit will give you the revelation. Either way, you will be doing something constructive about the situation. That is far better than spreading discord and, in essence, being the devil's tool.

Unbelief is a sin, and just like any other sin, there is a price to be paid. Because of their unbelief, the children of Israel wandered 40 years in an area that could have been crossed in 21 days. They simply could not find their way out. That is what sin will do to you. It will spiritually blind you.

You may think it is okay to gripe and complain because you do it and God does not strike you dead when you do it. But He has a lot of time. There is no hurry. He is not going anywhere — but you are. Payday is not every Friday, but payday is coming. It came for Israel. They got wiped out because of their complaining and because they would not take God at His Word.

4

Temptations, Trials, and Tests

We read in Hebrews 12:7 that we have a choice as to whether or not we endure chastening. We concluded from this that sickness, illness, and calamity could not be God's way of chastening us, because we have no choice when those things come upon us as to whether or not we wish to endure them.

The same could be said for temptations, trials, and tests. Some people have claimed through the years that God uses temptations and trials to train us. However, Jesus tells us this in Matthew 26:41:

> "Watch and pray, lest you enter into temptation. The spirit indeed is willing, but the flesh is weak."

If God uses temptations, trials, and tests to teach us or make us better, then something is wrong here. He is telling us to pray that we do not enter into temptation. If God sends temptation for us to enter into — because it is only as you enter into it that you are going to learn a lesson from it — then tells us to watch and pray that we do not enter into temptation, He is fighting against

Himself. If you do not enter in, how are you going to get the benefit of the lesson you would have received by entering into it?

First Corinthians 10:13 adds this:

> No temptation has overtaken you except such as is common to man;...

Notice, it does not say, "... common to Christians." It says, "... **common to man.**" These things come on everyone, saved or unsaved. What is God trying to teach the sinner? Nothing. Sinners are spiritually dead — in other words, cut off from God. You cannot teach the dead. The dead must become alive spiritually in order to teach them.

> No temptation has overtaken you except such as is common to man;...

Not common to Christians, but common to man. In other words, this kind of stuff happens to everyone. Christians are not the only ones who get sick. They are not the only ones who become impoverished. They are not the only ones who have automobile accidents or who are raped. Those kinds of things happen to everyone, so it could not be God's way of teaching His children.

> ... but God is faithful, who will not allow you to be tempted beyond what you are able, but with the temptation will also make the way of escape, that you may be able to bear it.

Escape means "to get away from." That sounds very similar to what Jesus told us in Matthew 26:41. If God sent calamities against you, He would want you to learn something from them. If He made a way of escape, you would escape not only from the temptation, trial, or test being placed before you, but from the lesson God was trying to teach you as well.

As we pointed out earlier, God teaches us by His Word. He does not want you to go through temptations, trials, and tests, and be bombed out by them. Those things come because the enemy brings them to destroy us. God brings us the way of escape so we can get out of those things. If you are obedient to the Word of God, there is always a way for you to escape.

God does not teach you through the circumstances. You can learn through circumstances, and maybe you did learn some things because your head was hard and your behind was soft, but that was because it was the only way you would learn. You would not listen to anyone, so you learned the hard way. Experience is definitely a teacher, but it is not the best one.

Let us say you see someone working in some sort of factory, and that person gets too close to a machine and gets his finger cut off. I would wager that the person who gets his finger cut off finds out that by getting too close to that machine, you can lose a limb. But that is not the best way for that person to learn. The best way for that person to learn is by obeying the sign which says, "Stay Behind the Red Warning Line."

You can learn some things by experience, but experience is not the best way. The best way to learn is by obeying God. If you obey God, there are many experiences you can avoid — because some of those experiences can kill you.

The Profit of the Word

We read 2 Timothy 3:16 earlier, but there is something in this verse which we did not mention before, which bears directly on what we are discussing now.

> **All Scripture is given by inspiration of God, and is profitable for doctrine, for reproof, for correction, for instruction in righteousness,**

Scripture is a synonym for the Bible — the Word of God. This verse says that all Scripture is given by inspiration of God and is profitable. Profitable means that it gives you some sort of benefit or gain, that it is advantageous for you to have. In short, you should be the better for having received it.

Hebrews 12:9-10 adds this:

> **Furthermore we have had human fathers who corrected us, and we paid them respect. Shall we not much more readily be in subjection to the Father of spirits and live?**
> **For they indeed for a few days chastened us as seemed best to them, but He for our profit, that we might be partakers of His holiness.**

Think about this: The first part of verse 10 says that our parents **chastened us as seemed best to them.**

However, this same verse says the reason God chastens us is **for our profit** — in other words, so that we will be the better.

Guarding Against Theft

No person is exonerated from temptations, trials, or tests. However, the one who is tempting, trying, and testing you is Satan, not God. Satan has one basic purpose in his mind for tempting, trying, and testing you. He does not want you to learn from God's Word how to live the God kind of life. He knows that if you find that out, you will put him to flight, and he will no longer be able to dominate you.

Satan brings trials, temptations, and tests upon you to steal the Word. Once he steals the Word, you will have no way to be chastened, and you will have no way to spiritually grow up and mature. In the process of doing this, the devil will blow your brains out, and take your money, your family, and anything else he can get his hands on, if he can get away with it. But his main purpose for coming is to separate you from the Word.

According to 2 Timothy 3:16, you profit by **all Scripture,** which **is given by inspiration of God.** By absconding with **all Scripture,** the devil gets away with the things that would profit you. This was what Jesus was getting at when He told the disciples the parable of the sower.

Mark 4:14-15:
  "The sower sows the word.

> "And these are the ones by the wayside where the word is sown. When they hear, Satan comes immediately and takes away the word that was sown in their hearts."

Satan does not wait until next week to come and take away the Word. He comes immediately.

Mark 4:16-17:

> "These likewise are the ones sown on stony ground who, when they hear the word, immediately receive it with gladness;
>
> "and they have no root in themselves, and so endure only for a time. Afterward, when tribulation or persecution arises for the word's sake, immediately they stumble."

Satan persecutes and tries to afflict you for the Word's sake. He does not come to persecute you through some strange person you do not know. He comes through relatives, friends, sometimes even your wife or your child. That is what makes persecution hurt, if you allow it to.

But you must do what Jesus said: "Father, forgive them." That is what I do all the time. I could let it bother me if someone who sits in the front row every week starts saying bad things about me, but I do not do that. I know it is not that person, but the devil. The person who talks about me does not really know me. If he really understood what he was doing, he would not say anything. Therefore, I just stay sweet, and say,

"Father, forgive him. He does not know what he is doing," because I am not going to let Satan steal my profit or my joy.

Mark 4:18-19:
"Now these are the ones sown among thorns; they are the ones who hear the word,

"and the cares of this world, the deceitfulness of riches, and the desires for other things entering in choke the word, and it becomes unfruitful."

You are not the one who becomes unfruitful. It is the Word that becomes unfruitful.

Mark 4:20:
"But these are the ones sown on good ground, those who hear the word, accept it, and bear fruit: some thirtyfold, some sixty, and some a hundred."

This is why you have to keep in mind the disparity between individuals. The Word is the same; therefore, conceivably, that Word should produce the same amount of harvest in the same amount of ground for everyone. But some people bring only thirty, some bring sixty, and others bring a hundredfold.

The ideal harvest would be a hundred. However, because of the difference in people in their levels of commitment, dedication, love, and desire, some bring thirty, and some bring sixty. The important thing is that at least they bring in the amount that they do, because the Word was sown in their hearts.

The Word does not work by itself. It does not matter how much Word you hear. It will not do you any personal good, nor will it have a positive affect on your life, unless you act upon it. There is a difference between thirty, sixty, and a hundred, but that difference is because of you, not because of the Word.

The Word will produce a hundred in every plot of ground — every life it touches — if allowed to. The catch is, you have to be willing for it to do that if you want it to manifest a hundred in your life.

Another very important benefit of the Word is stated in Ephesians 5:25-28:

> **Husbands, love your wives, just as Christ also loved the church and gave Himself for her,**
> **that He might sanctify and cleanse her with the washing of water by the word,**
> **that He might present her to Himself a glorious church, not having spot or wrinkle or any such thing, but that she should be holy and without blemish.**
> **So husbands ought to love their own wives as their own bodies; he who loves his wife loves himself.**

God cleanses us with **the washing of water by the word.** If you will listen to the Word, you will not have to learn through the circumstances. Satan will not have a way to get to you. He will not be able to put any temptation, trial, or test on you that will affect you, because you will be able to say, "I already know. I know what God said. I don't need to go through some foolishness that will keep me from attaining God's best."

A second scripture which refers to the cleansing power of the Word is John 15:1-3:

> "I am the true vine, and My Father is the vinedresser.
> "Every branch in Me that does not bear fruit He takes away; and every branch that bears fruit He prunes, that it may bear more fruit.
> "You are already clean because of the word which I have spoken to you."

This is the same thing Paul writes about in Ephesians. God uses His Word to cleanse us — if we submit to it.

Not Joyous Now, but Afterward ...

Once we submit to the Lord, sometimes the training can be hard. If you think back to your childhood, you may remember times when it seemed like your parents were trying to kill you, because the training they gave you was that rigid. However, you can look back on it now, and see that it was for your benefit. As Hebrews 12:11 puts it,

> Now no chastening seems to be joyful for the present, but painful; nevertheless, afterward it yields the peaceable fruit of righteousness to those who have been trained by it.

If it were trials, tribulations, and tests that chastened us, they would have the net result of making us righteous. But those things do not make you righteous. They make you hurt.

Also keep this in mind: What part of your three-fold nature is affected by temptations, trials, tests, sickness, disease, and poverty? It is your body. Of course, your soul, or your mind, can also be affected, because you have to think about the problems. But basically, tests and trials hit your body.

Notice what Hebrews 12:9 tells us.

> **Furthermore, we have had human fathers who corrected us, and we paid them respect. Shall we not much more readily be in subjection to the Father of spirits and live?**

Many Christians do not understand this verse. The first part of it says, **Furthermore, we have had human fathers.** Right away, the word *human* should alert us to the fact that God is going to show us a contrast between *human* and something else. Otherwise, you would not have to say *human*. What else would an earthly father be but human?

The contrast comes in the latter part of the verse, when Paul calls God **the Father of spirits.** The reason God is the Father of spirits is because we are spirits. God could not be called the Father of our flesh, because we are not flesh. He could not be the Father of our souls, because we are not souls. God is the Father of spirits. Jesus came to redeem spirits. When our spirits are redeemed, our bodies get to tag along for the ride.

Jesus says this in John 4:24:

"God is a Spirit, and those who worship Him must worship Him in spirit and truth."

God is a Spirit, and we are His children. If God is a Spirit, and we are His kids, we must also be spirits. A Black man and a Black woman coming together cannot produce a White baby. Two White people cannot come together and have an Asian child. Two Asians cannot come together and produce a Native American child. My point is, if God is our Father, we have to be whatever He is.

Since sickness, disease, trials, and tests affect your flesh, how can God use these things to train you when you are not flesh, but spirit? Cancer does not affect your spirit. Heart attacks do not affect your spirit. Tuberculosis does not affect your spirit. Not even AIDS or its complications affect your spirit. Therefore, God could not be the one using these things to train you, because you are a spirit, and nothing that God would do to your flesh would affect your spirit.

How does God contact, lead, and guide you, then? According to Proverb 20:27:

**The spirit of a man is the lamp of the Lord,
Searching all the inner depths of his heart.**

In other words, God will contact, lead, guide, train, and instruct you through your spirit, because that is the lamp He uses. Romans 8:16 confirms this by saying,

The Spirit Himself bears witness with our spirit that we are children of God,

God's Spirit does not bear witness with your flesh, or with your soul. It bears witness with your spirit. God trains and teaches us by His Word because His Word was designed for our spirits. As Jesus says in John 6:63,

"It is the Spirit who gives life; the flesh profits nothing. The words that I speak to you are spirit, and they are life."

He means that the words He speaks are addressed to your spirit, not to your flesh, your mind, or your soul. This is because God is the Father of spirits, and He uses His Word to train your spirit.

Blessed Is the Man Who Endures

In James 1:12, we are told:

Blessed is the man who endures temptation;...

That would sound sick if you did not understand what was happening. Why would a man be blessed if he endured temptation?

Just as we learned about chastening, the Greek word translated here as *endure* does not mean what you may think it means. In English, *endure* means "to sit quietly and put up with something." An example of this would be if you broke a tooth, and exposed a nerve. You would have to endure the pain and discomfort you would be experiencing — in other words, put up with it — until the dentist fixed your tooth.

In James 1:12, *endure* means something different. The word in that verse means you go through a situation, stand right in the midst of it, and are victorious over it. You come out better after it is over than you were before it started.

James 1:12-17:
> Blessed is the man who endures temptation; for when he has been approved, he will receive the crown of life which the Lord has promised to those who love Him.
>
> Let no man say when he is tempted, "I am tempted by God"; for God cannot be tempted with evil, nor does He Himself tempt anyone.
>
> But each one is tempted when he is drawn away by his own desires and enticed.
>
> Then, when desire has conceived, it gives birth to sin; and sin, when it is full-grown, brings forth death.
>
> Do not be deceived, my beloved brethren.
>
> Every good gift and every perfect gift is from above, and comes down from the Father of lights, with whom is no variation or shadow of turning.

All of this is tied in with temptation. Notice that every good gift and every perfect gift comes from God. Temptations, trials, and tests are not good, and they are not perfect. Sickness and disease are not good, and they are not perfect. Sin is not good, and it is not perfect. Therefore, none of these things come from God.

Every good gift comes down from God, from heaven. If every good gift comes down, every bad gift must come up from the pit, because "up" is the opposite of "down." God is sending down the good things, so Satan must be sending up the bad things.

Temptations, trials, and tests are bad, because they ravage your body. Your body is the temple of the Holy Ghost. Therefore, God will not create any condition that will have a negative affect on your body. This includes tumors, and any other malfunctions inside your body, especially ones that force the doctor to operate, and perhaps take out some organs to keep you alive.

If God were the cause of those malfunctions, He would be destroying His own temple. That would not make sense. God wants your body intact, every organ in place, every limb and member functioning as He designed it to operate — because your body is the place in which He dwells.

The chastening of the Lord is never bad, and it does not destroy or ravage you. It blesses you. You gain from it, because you learn how to win in life. For this reason, you should not resent it when our Heavenly Father tries to teach you. Rather, you should welcome it, because all you will do is succeed when you apply what you learn from God.

Once you make that application, you will love being chastened by the Lord. You will look forward to His instruction. And no matter what the enemy throws at you, if you remain true to God's teaching, you will always come out of the situation better than you were before you started. You will always win!

For a complete list of books and tapes by
Dr. Frederick K.C. Price, or to receive his publication,
Ever Increasing Faith Messenger, write

Dr. Fred Price
Crenshaw Christian Center
P.O. Box 90000
Los Angeles CA 90009

BOOKS BY FREDERICK K.C. PRICE, PH.D.

HIGH FINANCE
God's Financial Plan: Tithes and Offerings

HOW FAITH WORKS
(In English and Spanish)

IS HEALING FOR ALL?

HOW TO OBTAIN STRONG FAITH
Six Principles

NOW FAITH IS

THE HOLY SPIRIT —
The Missing Ingredient

FAITH, FOOLISHNESS, OR PRESUMPTION?

THANK GOD FOR EVERYTHING?

HOW TO BELIEVE GOD FOR A MATE

MARRIAGE AND THE FAMILY
Practical Insight For Family Living

LIVING IN THE REALM OF THE SPIRIT

THE ORIGIN OF SATAN

CONCERNING THEM WHICH ARE ASLEEP

HOMOSEXUALITY
State of Birth or State of Mind?

PROSPERITY ON GOD'S TERMS

WALKING IN GOD'S WORD
Through His Promises

PRACTICAL SUGGESTIONS FOR SUCCESSFUL MINISTRY

NAME IT AND CLAIM IT!
The Power of Positive Confession

THE VICTORIOUS, OVERCOMING LIFE
(A Verse-by-Verse Study of the Book of Colossians)

A NEW LAW FOR A NEW PEOPLE

THE FAITHFULNESS OF GOD

THE PROMISED LAND
(A New Era for the Body of Christ)

THREE KEYS TO POSITIVE CONFESSION

(continued on next page)

BOOKS BY FREDERICK K.C. PRICE, PH.D.

(continued)

THE WAY, THE WALK,

AND THE WARFARE OF THE BELIEVER

(A Verse-by-Verse Study of the Book of Ephesians)

BEWARE! THE LIES OF SATAN

TESTING THE SPIRITS

THE CHASTENING OF THE LORD

IDENTIFIED WITH CHRIST:

A Complete Cycle From Defeat to Victory

Available from your local bookstore

About the Author

Frederick K. C. Price, Ph.D., founded Crenshaw Christian Center in Los Angeles, California, in 1973, with a congregation of some 300 people. Today, the church's membership numbers well over 14,000 members of various racial backgrounds.

Crenshaw Christian Center, home of the renowned 10,146-seat FaithDome, has a staff of more than 200 employees. Included on its 30-acre grounds are a Ministry Training Institute, the Frederick K.C. Price III elementary, junior, and senior high schools, as well as the FKCP III Child Care Center.

The *Ever Increasing Faith* television and radio broadcasts are outreaches of Crenshaw Christian Center. The television program is viewed on more than 100 stations throughout the United States and overseas. The radio program airs on over 40 stations across the country.

Dr. Price has traveled extensively, teaching the Word of Faith simply and understandably in the power of the Holy Spirit. He is the author of several books on faith and divine healing.

In 1990, Dr. Price founded the Fellowship of Inner-City Word of Faith Ministries (FICWFM) for the purpose of fostering and spreading the faith message among independent ministries located in the urban, metropolitan areas of the United States.